T0208878

EPISTLES

BIBLESTUDY CROSSWORDS

BOB MEISTER

WestBow
PRESS®
A DIVISION OF THOMAS NELSON
& ZONDERVAN

Copyright © 2020 Bob Meister.

All rights reserved. No part of this book may be used or reproduced by any means, graphic, electronic, or mechanical, including photocopying, recording, taping or by any information storage retrieval system without the written permission of the author except in the case of brief quotations embodied in critical articles and reviews.

WestBow Press books may be ordered through booksellers or by contacting:

WestBow Press
A Division of Thomas Nelson & Zondervan
1663 Liberty Drive
Bloomington, IN 47403
www.westbowpress.com
1 (866) 928-1240

Because of the dynamic nature of the Internet, any web addresses or links contained in this book may have changed since publication and may no longer be valid. The views expressed in this work are solely those of the author and do not necessarily reflect the views of the publisher, and the publisher hereby disclaims any responsibility for them.

Any people depicted in stock imagery provided by Getty Images are models, and such images are being used for illustrative purposes only.
Certain stock imagery © Getty Images.

Scripture quotations taken from the New American Standard Bible® (NASB), Copyright © 1960, 1962, 1963, 1968, 1971, 1972, 1973, 1975, 1977, 1995 by The Lockman Foundation
Used by permission. www.Lockman.org

ISBN: 978-1-9736-8417-6 (sc)
ISBN: 978-1-9736-8416-9 (e)

Print information available on the last page.

WestBow Press rev. date: 02/19/2020

CONTENTS

CONTENTS

BIBLESTUDY CROSSWORDS

Learning God's Word!

"The Bible has been so many words to us – then all of a sudden the words become spirit and life because Jesus re-speaks them to us in a particular condition. That is the way God speaks to us, not by visions and dreams, but by words. When a man gets to God it is by the most simple way of words."

Oswald Chambers, "My Utmost for His Highest", January 3.

The purpose of BibleStudy CrossWords is to help us retain God's word and go deeper into its meaning. Our hope is that these puzzles will become tools to make scripture an integral part of your life and increase your faith in Jesus Christ.

BibleStudy CrossWords uses crossword puzzles to help people of any age learn God's word in more detail, increase retention and have fun doing it. Specific words from an NIV Bible form the answers to the across and down questions. Solving the puzzles is a three-step process:

1. Read the designated verses in an NIV Bible. If you take your time reading you will remember more detail; if you read more than once you will retain more of the storyline and specific words demanded by the puzzles. You will find that you read differently when reading to remember than just doing a casual read.

2. Select from the *Down* and *Across* questions you prefer based on how the puzzle is developing and fill in the answers as best you can. You may consider selecting questions that already have one or more letters filled in to help formulate a correct answer.

3. Check your answers with the NIV Bible after you have gone through all the questions. Every answer will consist of a specific word used in the designated Bible verse; read the corresponding verse and fill in the correct answer. This is the *study* part of BibleStudy CrossWords.

Bible Study

The EPISTLES puzzles provide opportunity for personal daily or weekly study. There are a variety of options for Bible study groups, one approach has each member reading the designated verses and solving the puzzles before coming to class to discuss selected questions, subject matter and context. Allowing time for summer vacations and holiday breaks, this approach provides a year's study of the Epistles.

ROMANS

Romans 3:27

"Where then is boasting? It is excluded.
By what kind of law? Of Works?
No, but by a law of faith." NASB

The book of Romans contains Paul's most comprehensive statement of the full meaning of the cross of Christ. Paul says, "For I am not ashamed of the Gospel, for it is the power of God for salvation to anyone who believes, to the Jew first, and also to the Greek."

From the very start, Paul develops the theme that all people are sinners and therefore need God's salvation. But how can this be done? Paul writes meticulously that the only way is through a personal relationship of faith and complete obedience to Jesus Christ. Salvation cannot come through human attempts to obey any law perfectly.

Then Paul explains what a new life in Christ entails. No longer does an individual have to live under the constant domination of sin, guilt and death. A believer is liberated by the Spirit of God and has inner peace, as well as peace with God. Paul goes to great lengths to expound God's original purpose in giving the law of Moses and how the Jews were part of God's master plan to bring all nations home through the grace provided by the cross of Jesus Christ.

Paul concluded with many practical things about how Christians should live in the world. We must serve one another. We must be good citizens. We must be tolerant and sensitive to the consciences of others. *NASB Key Word Study Bible*

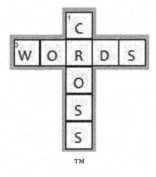

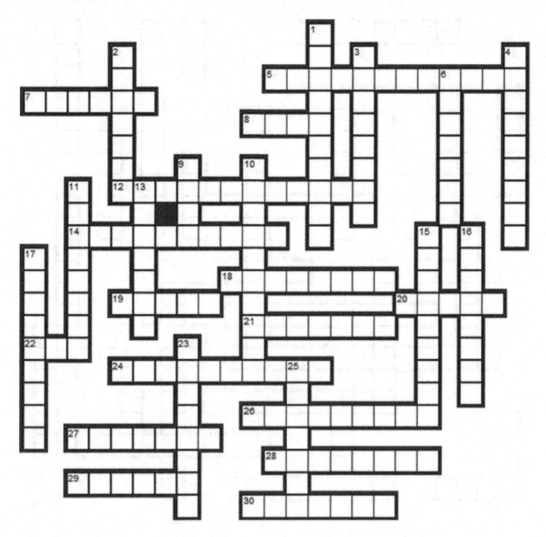

Across Romans 1-2

5. This had value only if you observed the law. 2:25
7. Men exchanged the glory of God for these. 1:23
8. Paul wrote to all in___ who were loved by God. 1:7
12. This event declared Jesus to be the Son of God. 1:4
14. God's kindness leads us toward this. 2:4
18. A man is a Jew if he is one___ by the Spirit. 2:29
19. Paul thanked God that the Romans had this. 1:8
20. God 's wrath is against those who suppress this. 1:18
21. What was Paul's calling? 1:1
22. Who did Paul serve with his whole heart? 1:9
24. God does not engage in this. 2:11
26. Men___ the truth of God for a lie. 1:25
27. God's role in Paul's devotion to the Romans? 1:9
28. Not knowing God leads to a___ mind. 1:28
29. What provides the power for salvation? 1:16
30. Sinful___ results in sexual impurity. 1:24

Down Romans 1-2

1. A word that describes men's indecent acts. 1:27
2. Men worshiped created things instead of the___1:25
3. There is no excuse to apply this against others. 2:1
4. How some women's relations are described. 1:26
6. Paul's relationship with Christ Jesus. 1:1
9. Men demonstrated this for one another. 1:27
10. As a human, Christ's relationship to David. 1:3
11. The state of men's foolish hearts. 1:21
13. Life that comes from God to those who do good. 2:7
15. God was not___ or thanked by men. 1:21
16. A consequence for those who do evil. 2:9
17. Paul's position to both Greeks and non-Greeks. 1:14
23. Paul asked a Jew, why not teach ___? 2:21
25. God will judge our___ through Jesus Christ. 2:16

Bible Study CrossWords

Romans 1-2

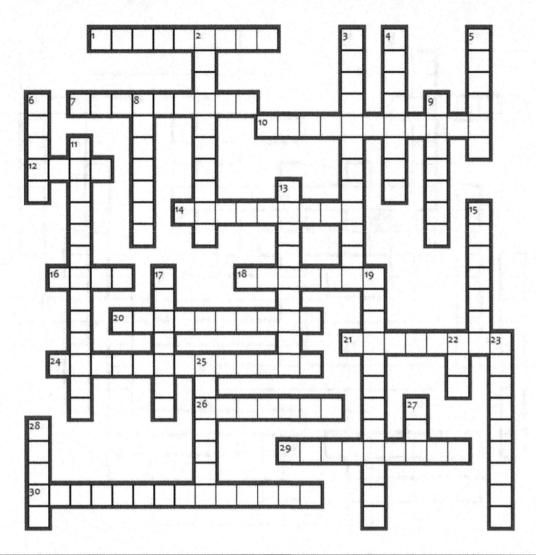

Across	Romans 3-4

1. Who received the promise with Abraham? 4:13
7. This comes from faith in the blood of Jesus. 3:25
10. The whole world is held____ to God. 3:19
12. While we are liars God remains ____. 3:4
14. Through the law we become____ of sin. 3:20
16. What does God give to the dead? 4:17
18. Abraham was made a father of many ____. 4:18
20. What wages should be considered to be. 4:4
21. God is the God of____ and Jews. 3:29
24. What from God is apart from the law? 3:21
26. Abraham was about this many years old. 4:19
29. Those who are sinners are ____. 3:7
30. We are blessed when these are forgiven. 4:7

Down	Romans 3-4

2. This comes by grace through Christ Jesus. 3:24
3. Abraham was faithful before this happened. 4:10
4. Faith excludes this. 3:27
5. What we did to fall short of the glory of God. 3:23
6. Without faith the law brings this. 4:15
8. Faith does not do this to the law. 3:31
9. Who is the father of the uncircumcised? 4:3
11. Jesus was raised to life for our ____ . 4:25
13. No one is considered to be this. 3:10
15. This is guaranteed to come through faith. 4:16
17. Righteousness comes to all who ____. 4:24
19. Against all hope Abraham was ____ in faith. 4:20
22. Faith is apart from observing this. 3:28
23. God presented Jesus as this. 3:25
25. Faith does this to the law. 3:31
27. Jews and Gentiles are both guilty of this. 3:9
28. A man is justified by this. 3:28

Bible Study CrossWords

Romans 3-4

Across   Romans 5-7

1. What was brought by the judgement? 5:16
5. Those who believe in God are credited with this. 5:24
6. What was in the world before sin? 5:13
8. The gift of God brought this to sinners. 5:16
10. The state of man when he is a slave to sin. 7:14
12. We are justified through this. 5:1
13. What is produced by perseverance? 5:4
15. When sinful nature dies, we are __from the law. 7:6
18. What does character produce?__. 5:4
19. What produces perseverance? 5:3
21. This should be an instrument for righteousness. 6:13
23. Our condition when Christ died for us. 5:8
24. The__ of Jesus saves us from God's wrath. 5:9
25. Who was a pattern for the one to come? 5:14
26. If we die with Christ we will__ with him. 6:8
27. The law has this only during our lifetime. 7:1
28. This is what we are to the one we obey. 6:16

Down   Romans 5-7

2. This from one man made many men righteous. 5:19
3. What kind of life is a gift through Jesus Christ? 6:23
4. From who does God's love come into our hearts? 5:5
7. To who should we offer ourselves for use? 6:13
9. When Jesus died to sin, he did it for how many? 6:10
11. The death of a sinner is considered to be this. 6:23
12. As slaves to righteousness we are__from sin. 6:18
14. It is through this we may be raised to a new life. 6:4
16. We are saved through the__ Jesus. 5:10
17. The law is___ because it helps us recognize sin. 7:14
20. Christ died for these people at just the right time. 5:6
22. What reigned from the time of Adam to Moses? 5:14

Bible Study CrossWords

Romans 5-7

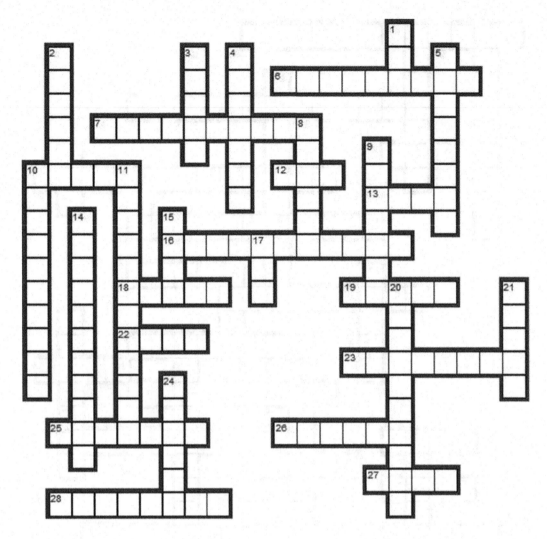

Across   Romans 8-10

6.   Not all who are____ from Israel are Israel. 9:6
7.   If we share this with Christ, we share in his glory 8:17
10.   The father of Rebekah's children. 9:10
12.   What caused God to send His Son as an offering? 8:3
13.   This is what causes God to work for our good. 8:28
16.   Paul thought of himself like sheep to be ____. 8:36
18.   We should use this to confess and be saved. 10:10
19.   God will apply this on whom He wants. 9:18
22.   A word that identifies God as Father. 8:15
23.   What waits in expectation for the sons of God? 8:19
25.   Isaiah said only these Israelites would be saved. 9:27
26.   If____ is in your body it is dead to sin. 8:10
27.   Those led by the Spirit have this relation to God. 8:14
28.   Christ was____to those who didn't ask for him. 10:20

Down   Romans 8-10

1.   Who should not talk back to God? 9:20
2.   Anyone who in Jesus will not be put to shame 10:11
3.   If we call on the name of the Lord we will be ___. 10:13
4.   If God is for us no one can be____ us? 8:31
5.   God called these people along with Jews. 9:24
8.   Who provides life and peace? 8:6
9.   It is with our hearts we____and are justified. 10:10
10.   What the Spirit does for the saints? 8:27
11.   The law of the Spirit sets us free from this. 8:1
14.   God did this to those He foreknew and called. 8:30
15.   God said He loved Jacob but not____. 9:13
17.   You will not sin if the Spirit of___ lives in you. 8:9
20.   We receive this through our adoption as sons. 8:23
21.   God was____ by those who did not seek Him. 10:20
24.   We should not live according to this nature. 8:12

Bible Study *CrossWords*

Romans 8-10

~ 8 ~

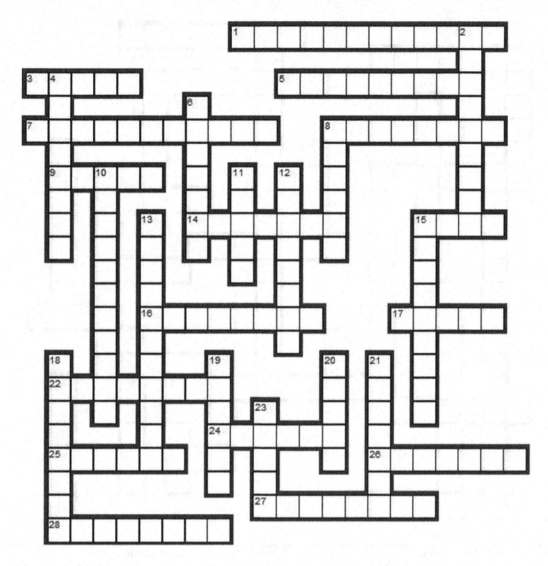

Across   Romans 11-13

1.   God has mercy on those bound to ____. 11:32
3.   Eventually all Israel will be ____. 11:26
5.   We can fulfill the law by loving our ____. 13:8
7.   God's gifts and his call are ____. 11:29
8.   Paul used these in a metaphor about salvation. 11:16
9.   The remnant of Israel was chosen by ____. 11:5
14.   We should not take this action with enemies. 12:19
15.   As Christians we are considered part of one ____. 12:5
16.   This happened to those not chosen by grace. 11:7
17.   We should do this with God's people in need. 12:13
22.   To whom should we pay our debts? 13:7
24.   Who appealed to God against Israel? 11:2
25.   God will do this to evil doers. 12:19
26.   The Gentiles salvation made Israel feel this way. 11:11
27.   God can treat us with both kindness and ____. 11:22
28.   Who should we love as we love ourselves. 13:9

Down   Romans 11-13

2.   We neither be proud nor this. 12:16
4.   From who does God's love come into our hearts? 5:5
6.   Christians do not conform to ____ of the world. 12:2
8.   Paul urged offering our ____ as living sacrifices. 12:1
10.   God established these as governing bodies. 13:1
11.   ____thousand Israelites did not bow to Baal .11:4
12.   Paul was the apostle to this group of people. 11:13
13.   This gift should be used in proportion to faith. 12:6
15.   The kind of love we should show to each other. 12:10
18.   Paul was an Israelite from this tribe. 11:1
19.   God did not do this to the people He foreknew. 11:2
20.   Regarding salvation Paul said this is nearly over. 13:12
21.   Our love for each other should be ____. 12:9
23.   According to grace, we each have different ____. 12:6

Bible Study
CrossWords

Romans 11-13

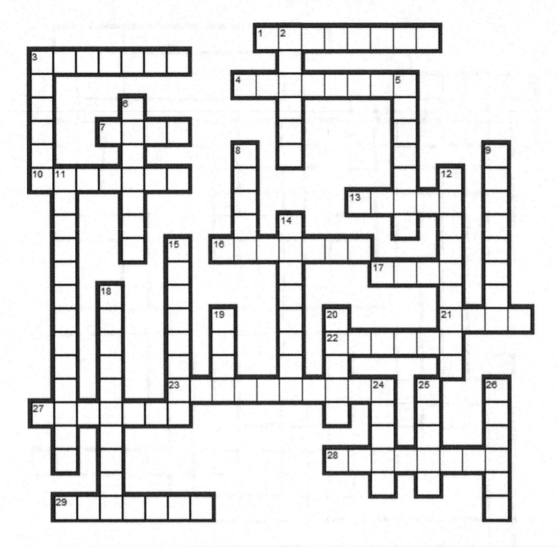

Across	Romans 14-16
1.	The strong should bear with the___ of the weak. 15:1
3.	Who was Paul's fellow worker? 16:21
4.	The___ were grateful to Priscilla and Aquila. 16:4
7.	Even those with___ faith should be accepted. 14:1
10.	Who was the director of public works? 16:23
13.	Satan will be crushed by the God of___. 16:20
16.	Christ absorbs the ___ intended for us. 15:3
17.	Paul said to greet one another with a holy ___. 16:16
21.	Whether dead or alive, who do we belong to? 14:8
22.	Who was a servant of the church in Cenchrea? 16:1
23.	Those who eat___should not look down on those who do not. 14:2
27.	Who wrote the letter for Paul? 16:22
28.	Paul asked for prayer because his___. 15:30
29.	Who was tested and approved in Christ? 16:10

Down	Romans 14-16
2.	Who along with Priscilla worked with Paul? 16:3
3.	Every knee will bow and every___will confess. 14:11
5.	People respect different days as___to the Lord. 14:6
6.	Criticizing what others eat can___ God's work. 14:20
8.	Who will soon be crushed by the God of peace? 16:20
9.	Who should we try to please and build up? 15:2
11.	God's kingdom is about___not about or differences in eating or drinking. 14:17
12.	Paul's next visit was to be to what city? 15:25
14.	We should pass___ on one another. 14:13
15.	Man must not condemn himself by what he ___. 14:22
18.	Do not pass judgment on these kinds of matters. 14:1
19.	Paul refers to God as being___. 16:27
20.	Where Paul planned to go after Jerusalem. 15:23
24.	Paul took___ in his service to God. 15:17
25.	We should not___or look down on our brother. 14:10
26.	We should___ one another as praise to God. 15:7

Bible Study CrossWords

Romans 14-16

CORINTHIANS

1 Corinthians 1:10

"Now I exhort you brethren, by the name of our Lord Jesus Christ,
that you all agree and there be no divisions among you, but
you be made complete in the same mind and in the same judgment." NASB

Corinth was one of the most prominent and prosperous cities during the time of Paul's missions. Generally, the people were intelligent and affluent, but arrogant and morally corrupt. They were struggling with many issues including idols, sex, marriage, and spiritual gifts and were experiencing conflicts over Christian freedom.

There came a point where a group of Christians wrote a letter to Paul asking him for his help solving their divided views on many issues. 1 Corinthians is his response, which emphasizes the need to be united in mind and thought on basic Christian beliefs beginning with the fact that Jesus Christ is Lord of all.

The second letter to the Corinthians challenges them to defend Paul and denounce false apostles who were trying to undermine him and distort his message. To help accomplish this Paul reminds them of his messages and his credentials that include his own persecutions.

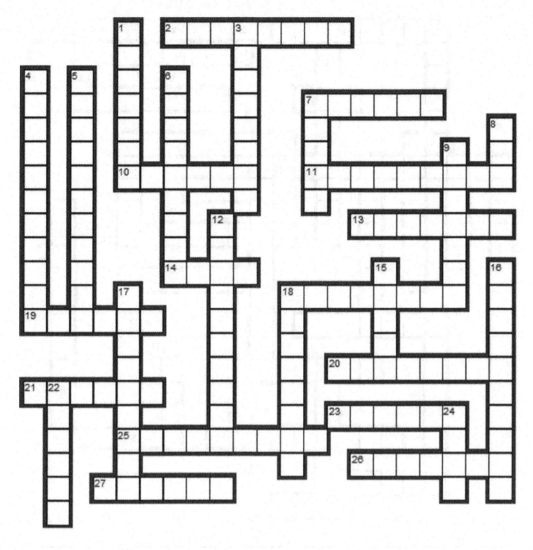

Across	1 Corinthians 1-3

2. Fellowship with Jesus is through God who is____. 1:9
7. What did Christ send Paul to preach? 1:17
10. Who searches the deep things of God? 2:10
11. Christians are united because Christ was____. 1:13
13. What things did God chose to shame the wise? 1:27
14. If we boast in whose name should we do it? 1:31
18. Paul told people they were not____ in his name. 1:13
19. Christ will keep us blameless and____ to the end. 1:8
20. Our minds are not capable to____ the Lord 2:16
21. Thoughts of us who think we are wise are ____. 3:20
23. Jews looked for signs and Greeks looked for this. 1:22
25. Paul appealed for agreement – not this. 1:10
26. Paul and____ considered themselves servants. 3:5
27. How Paul referred to God's wisdom. 2:7

Down	1 Corinthians 1-3

1. We should strive to be God's fellow ____. 3:9
3. Only the Spirit of God knows the____ of man. 2:11
4. The____ of God's is wiser than man's wisdom. 1:25
5. Paul asks where is the____ of this age? 1:20
6. This kind of man makes good judgements. 2:13
7. We receive this from God through Christ Jesus. 1:4
8. Who makes all things grow? 3:7
9. Paul does not want us to be____ in our faith. 1:13
12. Greeks look for wisdom and Jews demand these kinds of signs. 1:22
15. Since we are God's temple His Spirit____ in us. 3:16
16. God catches the wise in their ____. 3:19
17. Our____ is enriched because of God's grace. 1:5
18. As God's fellow workers we are also His____. 3:9
22. We should be perfectly____in mind and thought. 1:10
24. Paul said he gave this to early Christians because they were not ready for spiritual food. 3:4

Bible Study CrossWords

1 Corinthians 1-3

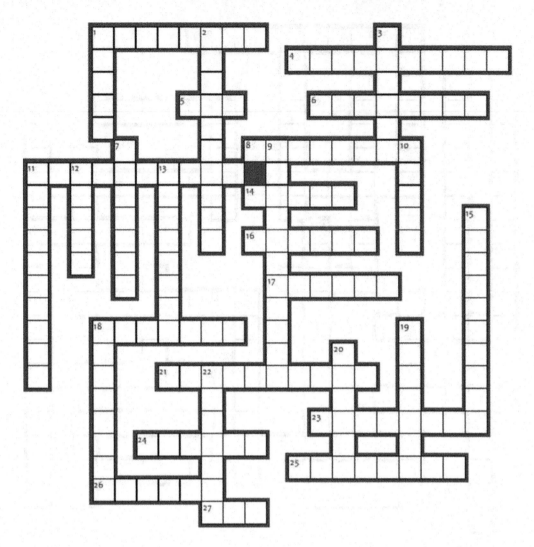

Across	1 Corinthians 4-6

1. Paul compares doing this to yeast in dough. 5:6
4. Apostles endured when this was done to them. 4:12
5. Who raised the Lord from the dead? 6:14
6. The apostles were treated in this way. 4:11
8. Who were considered fools for Christ? 4:10
11. Even though Paul was not___present he was able to judge the sexual immorality. 5:3
14. We should encourage this in comparing men. 4:6
16. The___ will not inherit the kingdom of God? 6:9
17. We should flee from this kind of immorality. 6:18
18. Paul urged people to___him. 4:16
21. This person will not inherit God's kingdom. 6:9
23. This is expected from someone trusted. 4:2
24. Our bodies are members of___. 6:15
25. Paul said he would not be___ by anything. 6:12
26. Our body is a___ of the Holy Spirit. 6:19
27. Paul referred to Timothy as a___. 4:17

Down	1 Corinthians 4-6

1. What apostles do when cursed. 4:12
2. There was sexual___ among Corinthians. 5:1
3. Paul wanted to represent this kind of spirit. 4:21
7. What man did Paul say he loved? 4:17
9. Paul said everything was___for him. 6:12
10. Who will destroy the sinful nature of man? 5:5
11. We should not unite our body with a ___.6:16
12. What works through the whole batch of dough? 5:6
13. Paul described some Corinthians as this. 4:18
15. For Paul all was permissible but not ___. 6:12
18. A clear conscience does not mean one is ___. 4:4
19. Who should not confront a___ in legality? 6:6
20. Even these men did not take their father's wife. 5:1
22. The Lord will judge men's ___. 4:5

Bible Study CrossWords

1 Corinthians 4-6

Across   1 Corinthians 7-9

2. Each person has their own____from God 7:7
4. Spouses should not____each other except by mutual consent. 7:5
8. An____man is concerned about the Lord's affairs. 7:32
9. It is better to marry than burn with . 7:9
10. A wife's____ does not belong to her alone. 7:4
11. A wife must not____ from her husband. 7:10
13. A woman is____ to her husband for life. 7:39
15. If the unbeliever does this let him do so. 7:15
17. Whose slave is he who is called by the Lord? 7:22
19. This should not be a stumbling block to the weak. 8:9
20. Don't do this to an ox while treading out grain. 9:9
22. We should become ____ to any man. 7:23
23. An____ husband is sanctified through his wife. 7:14
25. Husbands should fulfill this duty to their wives. 7:3
26. A wife's body also belongs to this person. 7:4
27. Love builds up, but what puffs up? 8:1
28. What was Paul compelled to preach? 9:16

Down   1 Corinthians 7-9

1. Paul had no commands for these women. 7:25
3. Those who marry will have many of these. 7:28
5. God has called us to live in ____. 7:15
6. A husband must do this to his wife. 7:11
7. Paul's____was sealed in the Lord. 9:2
12. Paul did not "____ " like an aimless runner. 9:26
14. Paul disciplined himself so that he would not be____when he preached. 9:27
15. But the man who____ God is known by God. 9:2
16. To avoid immorality each man should have his own ____. 7:2
18. What counts is to keep these that come from God 7:19
21. Paul won the Jews by being like a____. 9:20
24. An____ is nothing because there is just one God. 8:4

Bible Study
CrossWords

1 Corinthians 7-9

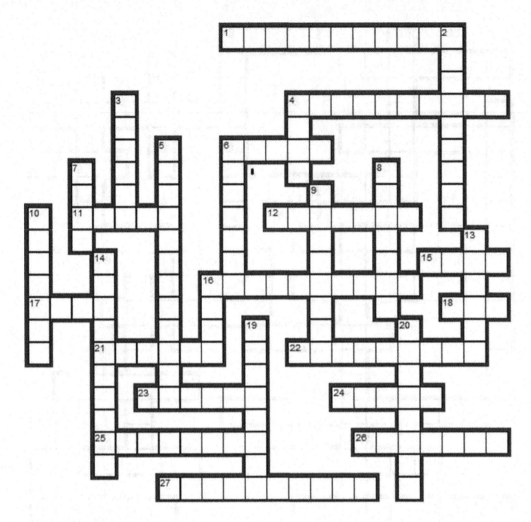

Across	1 Corinthians 10-11

1. We are being ___ by the Lord to avoid condemnation. 11:32
4. Everything is permissible but not ___. 10:23
6. What is the Lord's and everything in it? 10:26
11. Israel's forefathers were baptized into ___. 10:2
12. God was not ___ with most Israelites. 10:5
15. God was not ___ with most Israelites. 10:5
16. We should ___ the good of others. 10:24
17. This is common to all of man. 10:13
18. Woman is from man and man is ___ of woman. 11:12
21. Jesus said His body is for ___. 11:24
22. Who is the head of every man? 11:3
23. These people indulge in pagan revelry. 10:7
24. We should not commit ___ immorality. 10:8
25. Paul was critical of conduct at church meetings including being like this. 11:21
26. Jesus called His blood the new ___. 11:25
27. What things come from God? 11:12
26. Some participated in the Lord's Supper without___for others. 11:21
27. What things come from God? 11:12

Down	1 Corinthians 10-11

2. This should not exist between church members. 11:18
3. These people offer sacrifices to demons. 10:2
4. We cannot worship the Lord and demons ___. 10:21
5. Things permissible may not be ___. 10:23
6. A man should ___ himself before he eats of the bread and drinks of the cup. 11:28
7. For man did not ___ from woman. 11:8
8. One man's ___ shouldn't be judged by another's conscience. 10:29
9. This happened to Jesus at the Last Supper. 11:23
10. Some who did this were killed by an angel. 10:10
13. You can't drink the cup of the Lord and the cup of ___ too. 10:21
14. Our ___ should not be bothered by what we eat. 10:25
16. We should not do this to the Lord. 10:9
19. Paul said we should flee from this. 10:14
20. Some thought they were ___ firm against temptation when they were not! 10:12

Bible Study CrossWords

1 Corinthians 10-11

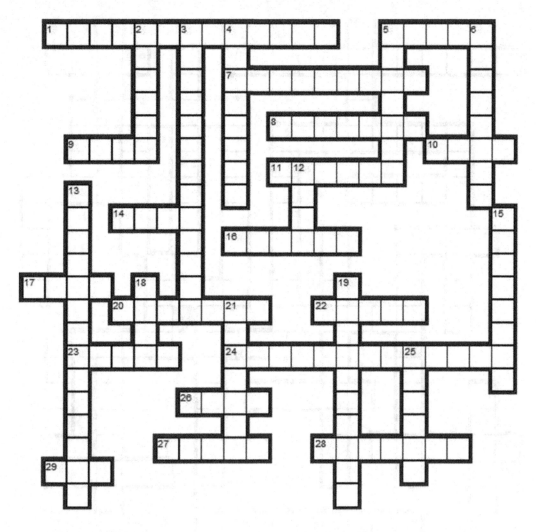

Across   1 Corinthians 12-14

1. Everyone receives the____ of the Spirit. 12:7
5. Love does not boast and is not ____. 13:4
7. The word of God did not____ with people. 14:36
8. If one body part is____then all others rejoice. 12:26
9. We should pray with this as well as our spirit. 14:15
10. What is one unit with many parts? 12:12
11. We are each part of whose body? 12:27
14. If you don't have this you are nothing. 13:2
16. This comes as a gift from the Spirit. 12:8
17. There are different gifts but the same___. 12:5
20. This type of speech is a Spiritual gift. 12:10
22. Love rejoices in this. 13:6
23. We should____ in gifts that build up the church. 14:12
24. Parts of the body that seem weak are ___. 12:22
26. Though made of many parts the body is a ___. 12:12
27. Love does not envy and does not ___. 13:4
28. Use all Spiritual gifts in a and orderly way. 14:40
29. Anyone who speaks in a tongue speaks to ___. 14:2

Down   1 Corinthians 12-14

2. Prophesy doesn't ___ speaking in tongues. 14:39
3. Spiritual gifts are for the ___of the church. 14:26
4. God's first appointments in the church. 12:28
5. Love is___as well as kind. 13:4
6. God is a God of peace – not___. 14:33
12. This body part is needed as much as the eye. 12:21
13. A gift of the Spirit is___of tongues. 12:10
15. The Spirit did this to make us into one body. 12:13
18. Of faith,___ and love, the greatest is love. 13:13
19. A Spiritual gift that edifies the church. 14:4
21. He who speaks in a tongue___himself. 14:4
25. Different kinds of gifts come from this source. 12:4

Bible
Study
CrossWords

1 Corinthians 12-14

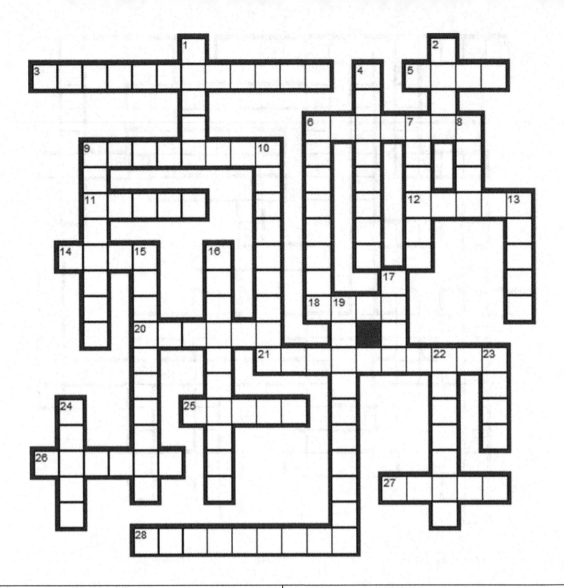

Across   **1 Corinthians 15-16**

3. Christ being raised from the dead proved this.15:13
5. This is sown in dishonor but raised in glory. 15:43
6. What will happen to us at the last trumpet? 15:51
9. Christ appeared to over five hundred of the___. 15:6
11. Christ gives us victory over the ___ of sin. 15:56
12. Christ first appeared to ___ before the Twelve. 15:5
14. Paul wanted greeting to be with a holy ___. 16:20
18. Each kind of___ has its own body. 15:38
20. Paul said donations should be based on this. 16:2
21. The nature of our bodies is___by God. 15:38
25. After the five hundred Christ appeared to___. 15:7
26. This happened to Christ on the third day. 15:4
27. How Paul rated himself as an apostle. 15:9
28. Doing this was useless if Christ was not raised. 15:14

Down   **1 Corinthians 15-16**

1. What is the last enemy to be destroyed? 15:26
2. Anyone who does not___the Lord is cursed. 16:22
4. Other than earthly bodies what kind are there? 15:40
6. What bad company does to good character. 15:33
7. What was the subject of Paul's preaching? 15:1
8. The first man was made from this. 15:47
9. If dead are not raised why are people ___? 15:29
10. Death has been___ up in victory. 15:54
13. Christ's___ will put his enemies under his feet. 15:25
15. What confirms that Christ died for our sins. 15:3
16. Paul refers to himself as being born in this way. 15:8
17. In Christ all are made alive, in this man all die. 15:22
19. What is it we should do in loving way? 16:14
22. Our bodies are sown as___ but raised spiritual. 15:44
23. What happens to a seed before it comes to life? 15:36
24. What caused Paul to work harder than others. 15:10

Bible Study CrossWords

1 Corinthians 15-16

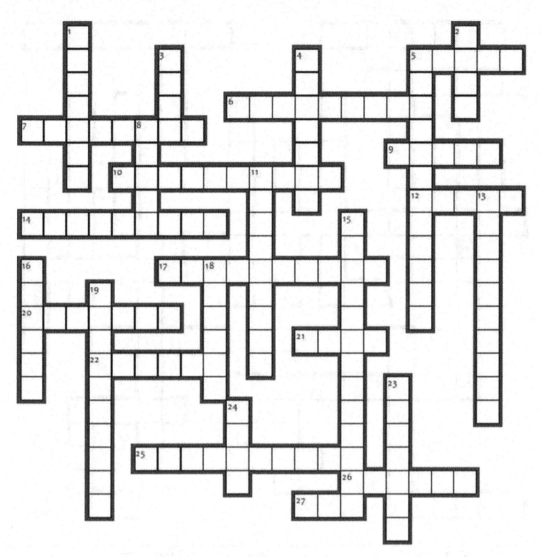

Across   2 Corinthians 1-3

5. The face of Moses reflected this. 3:7
6. Paul planned to visit Corinth on his way to __. 1:16
7. God did this to Paul & Timothy for their ministry. 1:21
9. It is by this that we stand firm in Christ. 1:24
10. God is the Father of__ and comfort. 1:3
12. Who was Paul looking for in Troas? 2:13
14. What kind of seal did God put on Paul? 1:22
17. Corinthians would endure the same__ as Paul. 1:7
20. Who was with Paul in Corinth? 1:1
21. Paul likens the word yes to this word. 1:20
22. Paul did not__ the word of God for profit. 2:17
25. Paul had __ that others would share his joy. 2:3
26. God put this in Paul's heart. 1:22
27. God's promises are always this in Christ. 1:20

Down   2 Corinthians 1-3

1. God provides this so we can provide it to others. 1:4
2. It was the hope of glory that caused Paul to be__. 3:12
3. This is provided to us by the Spirit. 3:6
4. This exists where the Spirit of the Lord is. 3:17
5. The Spirit was a deposit__what was to come. 1:22
8. Where did the Lord open a door for Paul? 2:12
11. Paul spoke before God with__. 2:17
13. Paul did not want Corinthians to be__ about his hardships. 1:8
15. The ministry of the Spirit brings this. 3:9
16. Paul called the Corinthians a__from Christ. 3:3
18. Paul called God the__of compassion. 1:3
19. Paul said his__ came from God. 3:5
23. Paul wrote in ___ to show the depth of his love. 2:4
24. Where did Paul and Timothy suffer hardships? 1:8

Bible Study
CrossWords

2 Corinthians 1-3

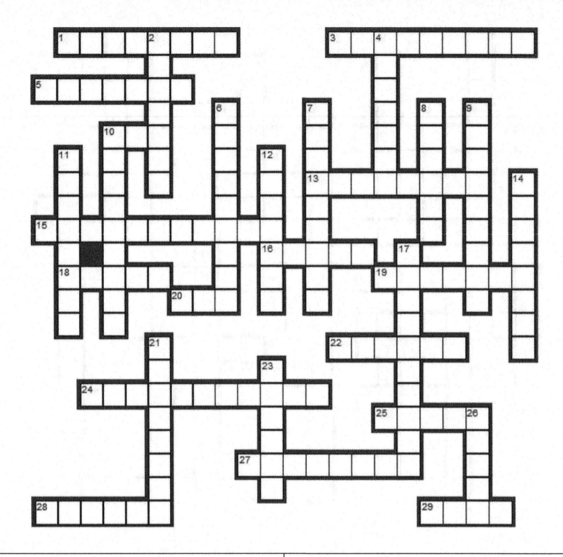

Across 2 Corinthians 4-6

1. Paul said this word represents the spirit of faith. 4:13
3. Paul renounced this as being shameful. 4:2

5. Outwardly we waste away but are ___ inside. 4:16
10. God made him who had no ___ to be sin for us. 6:21
13. Paul tried to do this because he feared the Lord. 5:11
15. Christ's ___ deliver the message of reconciliation. 5:20
16. Believers were told to not lose this. 4:16
18. Believers should live by ___ rather than by sight. 5:7
19. Paul did not use deception nor ___ God's word. 4:2
20. Who gave Paul the ministry of reconciliation? 5:18
22. Paul spoke openly and ___ to the Corinthians. 6:11
24. The god of this age has blinded the minds of ___ 4:4
25. Paul's ministry was possible through God's ___. 4:1
27. God created light to shine out of this ___. 4:6
28. A believer is created as the ___ of God. 6:16
29. Carrying the death of Jesus in our body helps to reveal the ___ of Jesus in us. 4:10

Down 2 Corinthians 4-6

What kind of house will believers have in heaven? 5:1
Paul said it was Christ's love that ___ he and Timothy in their ministry. 5:14
God's Spirit causes mortality to be ___ up by life. 5:4
What is unseen is eternal - what is seen is. 4:18
Our goal should be to ___ God. 5:9
Corinthians held this back from Paul and Timothy. 6:12
Paul said now is the time of favor and day of ___. 6:2
Paul renounced secret and ___ ways; 4:2
Paul and Timothy were hard pressed but not this. 4:8
God's reconciliation makes believers a new ___. 5:17
Being yoked to unbelievers is being yoked to ___. 6:14
Knowledge from God is like having this in a jar. 4:7
There is no harmony between Christ and ___? 6:15
We should not be ___ with unbelievers. 6:14

Bible Study CrossWords

2 Corinthians 4-6

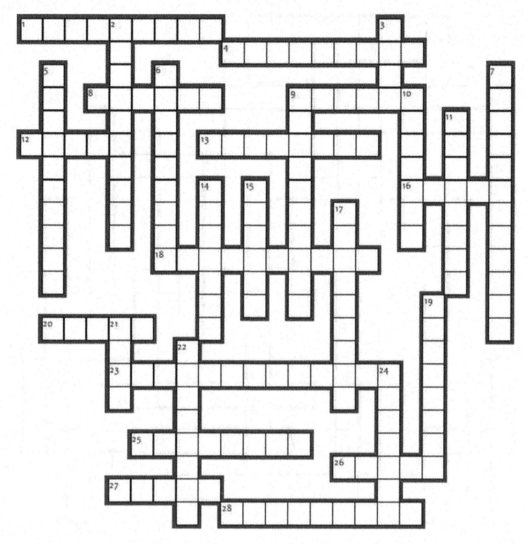

Across 2 Corinthians 7-10

1. This describes Corinthian's attitude to service. 9:2
4. Godly sorrow and repentance lead to this. 7:10
8. Paul asked for the Corinthians to make room for him and the others in their____. 7:2
9. Who did Paul call meek and gentle? 10:1
12. One should give what he decides in his to give. 9:7
13. Christ was described as having this characteristic.10:1
16. This comes from excelling in giving. 8:7
18. God had given grace to these churches. 8:1
20. Paul's standards were different than the____. 10:2
23. God's____endures forever. 9:9
25. Paul claimed this happened to them at every turn. 7:5
26. We should not do this beyond proper limits. 10:13
27. Paul was comforted by the coming of this person. 7:6
28. This happened to the spirit of Titus. 7:13

Down 2 Corinthians 7-10

1. Paul was happy because their sorrow led to this. 7:9
3. Who does this sparingly will reap sparingly. 9:6
5. Giving willingly makes a gift____. 8:12
6. Paul wanted to avoid this regarding his offering. 8:20
7. Paul was ready to punish every act of ___. 10:6
9. Paul had great____ in the Corinthians. 7:16
10. We must take this captive to be obedient. 10:5
11. Proper giving was necessary to produce this. 8:13
14. Titus shared this feeling for the Corinthians. 8:16
15. This kind of sorrow brings death. 7:10
17. God has____ abroad his gifts to the poor. 9:9
19. Corinthians had proved themselves to be ___ in the matter of repentance. 7:11
21. In whose name should we boast. 10:17
22. What should be our attitude when giving? 9:7
24. Some were looking just on the ___ of things. 10:7

Bible Study CrossWords

2 Corinthians 7-10

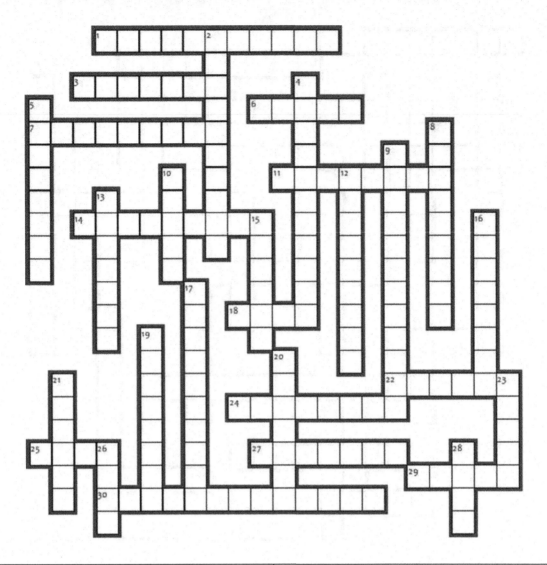

Across　　　　2 Corinthians 11-13

1. Satan____ as an angel of light. 11:14
3. Do we____ that Christ Jesus is in us? 13:5
6. Paul's torment is described as a____. 12:7
7. This was given to Paul from the Lord. 13:10
11. Paul boasted in things that showed this. 11:30
14. Men from here supplied what Paul needed. 11:9
18. Paul said to greet each other with a holy____. 13:12
22. For whose sake did Paul delight in weakness? 1210
24. Paul's concern for churches caused this daily. 11:28
25. Paul warned not to think of him as this. 11:16
27. Paul____ and toiled without sleep. 11:27
29. We should test ourselves to see if we have this. 13:5
30. What Paul did was for____ the Corinthians. 12:19

Down　　　　2 Corinthians 11-13

2. Paul said he would gladly spend this for Corinthians. 12:15
4. Paul did not want the Corinthians'____. 12:14.
5. The third heaven is the same as ____. 12:4
8. Every matter should be tested by this. 13:1
9. Things that mark an apostle are done with ____. 12:12
10. Paul said his jealousy was ____. 11:2
12. Paul was not a great speaker, but he had this. 11:6
13. Paul gave this to the Corinthians twice. 13:2
15. No one from here would stop Paul's boasting. 11:10
16. Where was Paul arrested? 11:32
17. Corinthians were told to aim for this. 13:11
19. Paul was not ____ to "super-apostles." 11:5
20. Paul preached the Gospel to____ the Corinthians. 11:7
21. Christ's power made Paul____when weak. 12:10
23. We must be for this not against it. 13:8
26. If I love you more, will you love me ____? 12:15
28. How many times did Paul get "40 lashes minus one"? 11:24

Bible Study

CrossWords

2 Corinthians 11-13

GALATIANS

Galatians 5:1

"It was for freedom that Christ set us free;
therefore, keep standing firm and do not
be subject to a yoke of slavery." NASB

Paul wrote to deny the legality which was the premise of the old covenant and promote freedom from the law by the atonement of Christ as established in the new covenant.

Jewish teachers were insisting that the only path to salvation was adherence to Mosaic law, including the ritual of circumcision, setting up the conflict of legalism versus faith. Paul taught that salvation came from God's grace through repentance and faith in Jesus Christ as Lord and Savior.

Jews in Galatia were also attacking Paul personally to discredit him and minimize his influence. He defends his authority as an apostle of Jesus Christ having received it directly from God and confirmed by the endorsement of James, Peter, and John.

He reaffirms that we receive the Holy Spirit through faith in Jesus Christ and that true Christian freedom requires living by the Spirit and fulfilling the law of Christ. It is the Holy Spirit who guides us and provides the power we need to overcome evil desires.

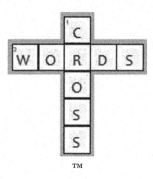

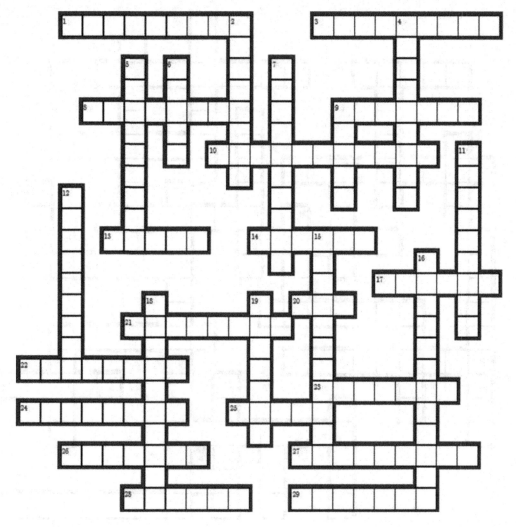

Across   **Galatians 1-3**

1.   We are not____ by following the law. 2:16
3.   All who rely on____ the law is under a curse. 3:10
8.   Who came to Jerusalem with Paul and Titus? 2:1
9.   How many days did Paul stay with Peter? 1:18
10.   Our faith replaces the____ of the law. 3:25
13.   Who sent Paul to the Galatians? 1:1
14.   Peter forced Gentiles to follow these customs. 2:14
17.   We don't receive the____by following the law. 3:2
20.   Paul was not trying to please____. 1:10
21.   We are____ because Christ became a curse for us. 3:13
22.   To who was Paul entrusted to preach the Gospel? 2:7
23.   Where did Paul oppose Peter? 2:11
24.   God does not judge by____ appearance. 2:6
25.   We cannot reach our goals by this kind of effort. 3:3
26.   Before God's call Paul was focused on this. 1:13
27.   Paul accused the Galatians of____ the Gospel. 1:6
28.   Who put the law into effect? 3:19
29.   Paul was____ to the Christian churches in Judea. 1:22

Down   **Galatians 1-3**

2.   Where did Paul go from Arabia? 1:17
4.   These people live by faith not by the law. 3:11
5.   What told Gentiles they would be justified by faith? 3:8
6.   Abraham received his inheritance through God's____. 3:18
7.   Before Paul's faith he did this to God's church. 1:13
9.   What saves us in Christ Jesus. 2:16
11.   Christ lived in Paul because he was____ with Him. 2:20
12.   Galatians experienced this because of false preaching. 1:7
15.   God gave Abraham this through a promise. 3:18
16.   This group caused Peter's separation from Gentiles. 2:12
18.   In what way did Paul receive the Gospel? 1:12
19.   Paul's prior attitude about Jewish traditions. 1:14

Bible Study CrossWords

Galatians 1-3

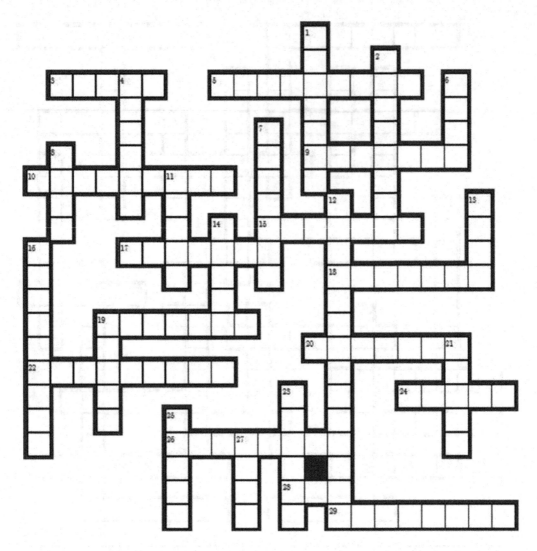

Across	**Galatians 4-6**
3.	False teaching is compared to using this in baking. 5:9
5.	We should be led by the Spirit to not act like this. 5:26
9.	Acts of the sinful nature are____. 5:19
10.	In Christ we have done this to the sinful nature. 5:24
15.	Because of this Paul first preached the Gospel. 4:13
17.	We can be like this if the purpose is good. 4:18
18.	Don't use your freedom to____ the sinful nature. 5:13
19.	Paul feared he had wasted this on Galatians. 4:11
20.	We should carry the____of each other. 6:2
22.	Those justified by law are____from Christ. 5:4
24.	We should not become____while doing good. 6:9
26.	If we belong to Christ whose seed are we. 3:29
28.	How many sons did Abraham have? 4:22
29.	Who should we love as we love ourselves? 5:14

Down	**Galatians 4-6**
1.	It is for this that Christ has set us free. 5:1
2.	He who overrates himself____ himself. 6:3
4.	If we are led by the this we are not under law. 5:18
6.	We were redeemed to have the rights of____. 4:5
7.	A son of Abraham was born because of this. 4:23
8.	Children of promise are born of the____ woman. 4:31
11.	Who was a child of promise. 4:28
12.	In Christ Jesus this does not have value. 5:6
13.	Our faith should be expressed in this way. 5:13
14.	We should do this only in the cross of Christ. 6:14
16.	The free and slave women represented two ____. 4:24
19.	Paul asked if he became this by telling the truth? 4:16
21.	One of Abraham's sons was born by a____woman? 4:223
23.	God sent the Spirit of his Son into Christians'____. 4:6
25.	bore children who were to become slaves. 4:25
27.	The Spirit calls out____ Father. 4:6

Bible Study CrossWords

Galatians 4-6

EPHESIANS

Ephesians 4:4-6

"There is one body and one Spirit, just as also you were called
in one hope of your calling. One Lord, one faith, one
baptism, and one God and Father of all who is over all and
through all and in all." NASB

Paul wrote this letter after he had established the church in Ephesus and returned a year later to stay for three more years. That gave him opportunity to have an effective influence through preaching the gospel. For that reason, this letter delivered by Tychicus was not so much to instruct as it was to explain the nature of the church as the body of Christ and the importance of having unity in their commitment to Christ and their use of Spiritual gifts.

Paul likens unity within the church body to family life and the respect that should be demonstrated.

"Children obey your parents in the Lord, for this is right.
Honor your father and mother,
which is the first commandment with a promise." NASB 6:1-3

Great emphasis is placed on the value of our relationship with the Holy Spirit and the importance of his influence on how we should treat others.

"And do not grieve the Holy Spirit of God, by whom you were sealed
for the Day of redemption. Let all bitterness and wrath
and anger and slander be put away from you, along with all malice."
NASB 4:30-31

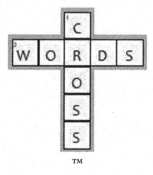

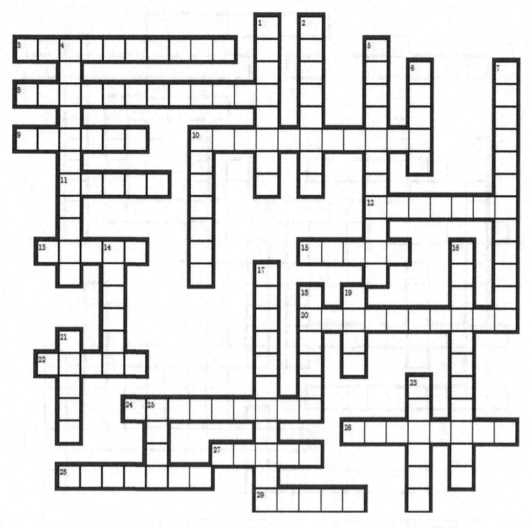

Across   Ephesians 1-3

3. The blood of Jesus Christ provides this to us. 1:7
8. Paul had grace to preach the___riches of Christ. 3:8
9. Paul said the faithful are___in Christ. 1:11
10. We have this in accordance with God's grace. 1:7
11. Raised from the dead, Christ sits at God's ___hand. 1:20
12. Paul had special___ into the mystery of Christ. 3:4
13. God who loves us is rich in this. 2:4
15. In respect Paul did this before God the Father. 3:14
20. Christ was appointed to be head over this. 1:22
22. Without Christ we are by nature objects of this. 2:3
24. God chose us in Christ to be___. 1:4
26. Paul considered himself a _ of Jesus Christ. 3:1
27. Through this we can approach God in confidence. 3:12
28. The fulfillment of God's will is described as this. 1:9
29. Our redemption is to the praise of God's ___. 1:14

Down   Ephesians 1-3

1. God applied this when raising Jesus from the dead. 1:19
2. Those who did this were marked with a seal. 1:13
4. Paul's asked people not to be___ by his suffering. 3:13
5. In love God___us to be His sons through Jesus Christ. 1:5
6. Paul said he was the___ of all God's people. 3:8
7. The Holy Spirit is a deposit ___ our inheritance. 1:14
10. With faith in Jesus we can approach God with this. 3:12
14. Who is head of all things in heaven and on earth? 1:10
16. The eyes of our hearts should be___ in hope. 1:18
17. Paul was doing this for the Galatians in his prayers. 1:16
18. God has blessed us in the heavenly ___. 1:3
19. God placed all things under Christ's ___. 1:22
21. This is the Gospel of our salvation. 1:13
23. Paul was a servant of___by the gift of God's grace. 3:7
25. Christ's___surpasses knowledge. 3:19

Bible Study CrossWords

Ephesians 1-3

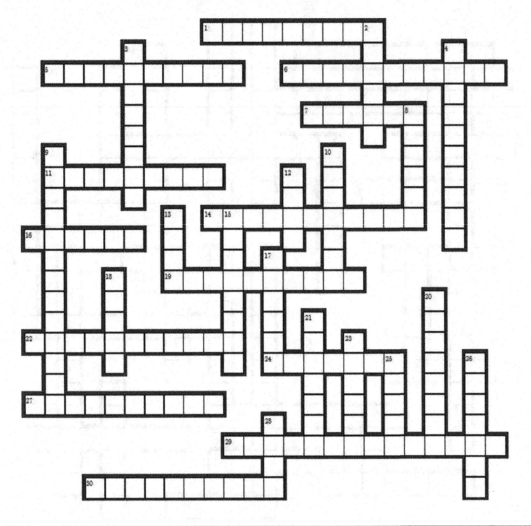

Across   Ephesians 4-6

1. As His children we should be____ of God. 5:1
5. We should get rid of this and all rage and anger. 4:31
6. God's wrath comes on those who are ____. 5:6
7. Husbands should love wives as they love their____. 5:28
11. We must avoid____, foolish talk, and coarse joking. 5:4
14. Christ has given each of us grace in this way. 4:7
16. God wants us to be____ in the fullness of Christ. 4:13
19. Fathers should not do this to their children. 6:4
22. Don't let this kind of talk come from your mouth. 4:29
24. God our Father is over all, in all and____ all. 4:6
27. The Gentiles had given themselves up to this. 4:19
29. We should serve men____ just as we serve God. 6:7
30. Impurity, greed and sexual____are improper. 5:3

Down   Ephesians 4-6

2. What wives should do with their husbands. 5:22
3. Paul cautioned not to live as these people did. 4:17
4. The Holy Spirit of God seals us for the day of____. 4:30
8. We should stand firm and take up the ____ of faith 6:16
9. When forgiving each other we should be____. 4:32
10. We should be ____, humble and gentle with others. 4:2
12. We should serve others as we serve our____. 6:7
13. We should imitate God by living a life of ____. 5:2
15. Paul thought of himself as a____of the Lord. 4:1
17. This and a sword are said to represent salvation. 6:17
18. The____ of God protects against the devil. 6:11
20. Christ's ascension above the heavens filled this. 4:10
21. Christ prepared us for different works of____. 4:12
23. We should be patient, gentile, and____. 4:2
25. Parents should receive this from their children. 6:2
26. Truth, as part of the armor of God is a belt____around our waist. 6:14
28. There is one____just as there is one Spirit, one Lord, one faith, one baptism, one God and Father. 4:4

Bible Study CrossWords

Ephesians 4-6

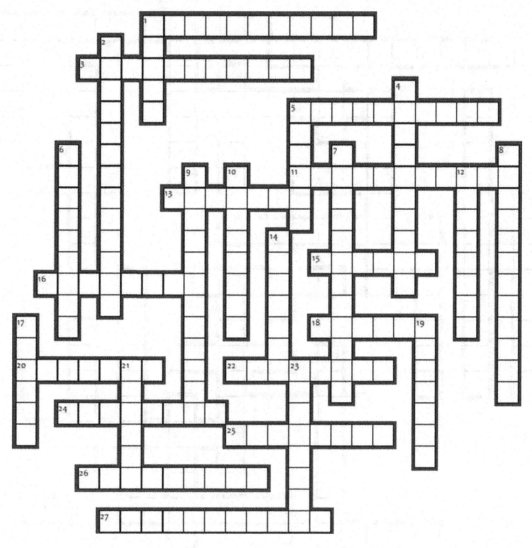

Across   **Philippians**

1. What happened to Paul was for his____1:19
3. This describes our residence in heaven. 3:20
5. We should display this characteristic to all. 4:5
11. Paul's relationship with Philippians was a____. 1:5
13. Paul was chained for his____of the gospel. 1:16
15. Paul desired to____ and be with Christ. 1:23
16. Paul said, "I thank God every time I____you." 1:3
18. Paul considered his____a loss for the sake of Christ. 3:7
20. Paul thought being in prison would____ the gospel. 1:12
22. Most important to Paul was that Christ be ____. 1:18
24. Who looks out for his own interests before Christ's? 2:21
25. Our____toward others should be the same as Christ Jesus. 2:5
26. We should have the same____as Jesus Christ. 2:21
27. Stopping this will help us become children of God. 2:14

Down   **Philippians**

1. Paul was poured out like this kind of offering. 2:17
2. These did not affect Paul's contentment. 4:11
4. Paul believed God had called him____in Christ Jesus. 3:14
5. We should conduct ourselves to be worthy of this. 1:27
6. Paul prayed the Philippians would become this. 1:10
7. We should think about these kinds of things. 4:8
8. Who did Paul want to send back to Philippi. 2:25
9. The power of Jesus Christ is found in this. 3:10
10. What tribe was Paul from? 3:5
12. This trait reflects consideration for others. 2:3
14. Paul was wanted others to____with him. 2:18
17. These helped Paul encourage others in Christ. 1:14
19. Who did Paul hope to send to the Philippians? 2:19
21. Paul said to live is ____ and to die is gain. 1:21
23. We should do nothing out of __ or vain conceit. 2:3

Bible Study CrossWords

Philippians

~ 31 ~

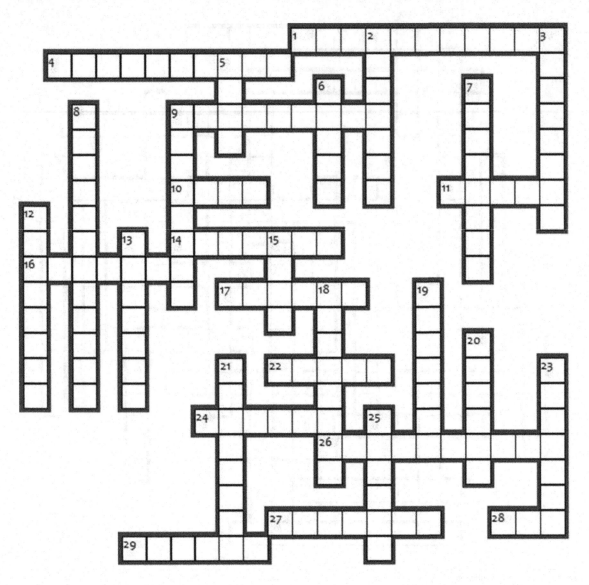

Across   **Colossians**

1. Who was Pauls' fellow prisoner? 4:10
4. The Gospel that has been___ to every creature. 1:23
9. Christ is the___ of the dead. 1:18
10. What binds all virtues together? 3:14
11. We must not do this based on what someone eats. 2:16
14. We should not set our minds on these things. 3:2
16. Who was asked to treat slaves in a fair way? 4:1
17. This should be done while watchful and thankful. 4:2
22. God made us___ with Christ. 2:13
24. Where all the grace of the deity lives. 2:9
26. In what things should children obey their parents? 3:20
27. All things were___ by and for the Son. 1:16
28. We should not do this to each other. 3:9
29. Christ was___ all things. 1:17

Down   **Colossians**

2. We must rid ourselves of___ and filthy language. 3:8
3. Paul did this for the church body. 1:24
5. Who was the cousin of Barnabus? 4:10
6. Where was the gospel growing and fruitful? 1:6
7. Wisdom and knowledge are___hidden in Christ. 2:3
8. This should always be full of grace. 4:6
9. The___ of the deity lives in Christ. 2:9
13. God commissioned Paul to be a___of the church. 1;25
15. Christ holds this position in the body of the church. 1:18
18. Fathers should not do this to children. 3:2
19. Who visited the Colossians with Paul? 1:2
20. We must___ourselves with gentleness and patience. 3:12
21. Before Christ this made men enemies of God. 1:22
23. We should do this for others as God does for us. 3:13
25. We should set our___ on things above where Christ is. 2:18

Bible Study CrossWords

Colossians

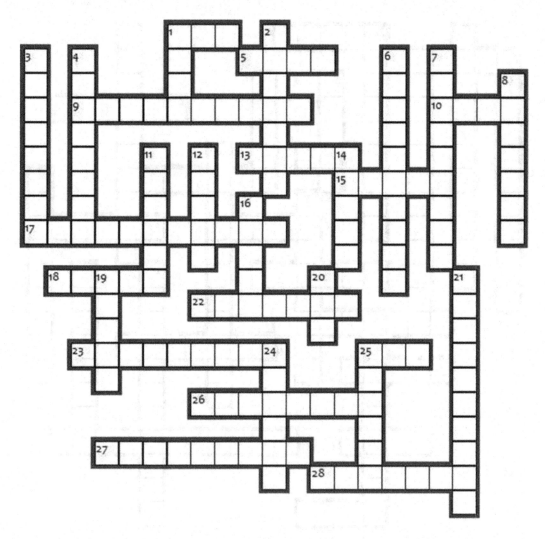

Bible Study
CrossWords

1 Thessalonians

Across   1 Thessalonians

1.   Paul's message was welcomed with___. 1:6
5.   To stand firm in the Lord is to really ___. 3:8
9.   Paul delivered the Gospel despite this. 2:2
10. This should increase in us and overflow. 3:12
13. The day of the Lord will come like a ___. 5:2
15. We should be___ and self-controlled. 5:6
17. What will come suddenly like labor pains? 5:3
18. Who rescues us from the coming wrath? 5:9
22. How long will the resurrected be with the Lord? 4:17
23. Thessalonians' faith was an influence in this place. 1:7
25. Who taught us about brotherly love? 4:9
26. Where did Paul suffer and was insulted? 2:2
27. Whose voice will represent the call of God? 4:16
28. The living will not___the dead in resurrection. 4:15

Down   1 Thessalonians

1.   They tried to keep Paul from speaking to Gentiles. 2:14
2.   Who brought the good news of faith and love? 3:6
3.   How did God feel about Paul preaching the Gospel? 2:4
4.   How did Paul refer to the men in Thessalonica? 1:4
6.   We should not treat these with contempt. 5:20
7.   God appointed us to receive this through Christ. 5:9
8.   We should show this to those who admonish us. 5:12
11. Where will the resurrected meet the live faithful? 4:17
12. Our ambition should be to lead this kind of life. 4:11
14. Timothy was sent to strengthen and encourage____ . 3:2
16. The Gospel gets this from the Holy Spirit. 1:5
19. Who stopped Paul from visiting when in prison? 2:18
20. Paul did not look for praise from these people. 2:6
21. It is God's will that this should happen to us. 4:3
24. God brings with Jesus believers in this condition. 4:14
25. We should not do this like men who have no hope. 4:13

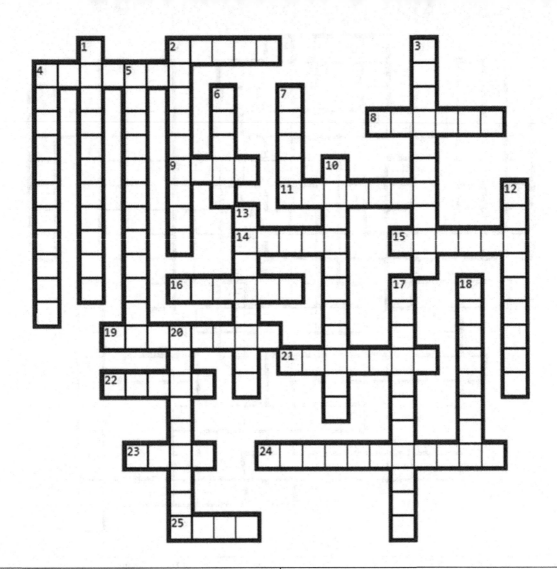

Across	2 Thessalonians
2.	We are saved by loving this. 2:10
4.	Paul said Thessalonians should follow his__. 3:7
8.	Paul didn't eat anyone's food without__ for it. 3:8
9.	Keep away from everyone you consider is this. 3:6
11.	Paul asked that the Lord's word would be__. 3:1
14.	Never tire of doing what is considered to be this. 3:13
15.	The lawless one will set himself up in this place. 2:4
16.	Through this we will share in the glory of Jesus. 2:14
19.	The lawlessness one must be __before Christ returns 2:3
21.	Paul worked hard doing this not to be a burden. 3:8
22.	Paul blessed them with this from the Lord Jesus. 3:18
23.	We are told to do this in order to deserve to eat. 3:10
24.	We are saved through this work of the Spirit. 2:13
25.	Idle people should__ the bread they eat. 3:12

Down	2 Thessalonians
1.	This secret power is already at work. 2:7
2.	The brothers were told to follow this from Paul. 2:15
3.	These people should work and earn their bread. 3:11
4.	Not knowing God brings this kind of destruction. 1:9
5.	Obedience brings God's love and Christ's __. 3:5
6.	The lawless one will do this to himself. 2:4
7.	Paul boasted about the Thessalonians' __. 1:4
10.	Disobeying Paul's__ resulted in shame. 3:14
12.	Jesus will do this to the lawless one. 2:8
13.	Paul said not to be confused by some __, 2:2
17.	Satan will display these types of miracles. 2:9
18.	God sends this to those who believe the lie. 2:11
20.	Paul prayed God to do this to their hearts. 2:17

Bible Study CrossWords

2 Thessalonians

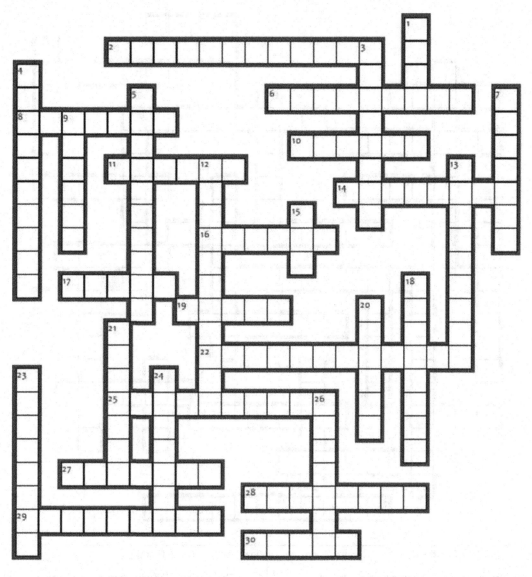

Across   1 Timothy

2. This act helps women to be saved. 2:15
6. Who had his faith shipwrecked? 1:20
8. What did we bring into the world? 6:7
10. One must manage this before managing a church. 3:4
11. We should not put our hope in this. 6:17
14. Children practice this by caring for their family. 5:4
16. God is this to all of us. 4:10
17. We should avoid this during prayer. 2:8
19. This describes the task of an overseer. 3:1
22. All God created should be received with this. 4:4
25. To what does God give life? 6:13
27. Paul says that Godliness is a____ 3:16
28. How were women instructed to dress? 2:9
29. How does Paul describe the patience of Jesus? 1:16
30. Men were teaching this kind of doctrine____1:3

Down   1 Timothy

1. What comes from a pure heart and sincere faith? 1:5
3. Paul was appointed to teach these people. 2:7
4. What Jesus did before Pontius Pilate. 6:13
5. Not caring for our family is worse than an ____. 5:8
7. We are told to repay these people. 5:4
9. Men must be___ before becoming a deacon. 3:10
12. The wife of a deacon must be___ 3:11
13. Paul wants men to pray without___, 2:8
15. Who is the blessed and only ruler? 6:15
18. What Jesus is between us and God? 2:5
20. Who says that some of us will abandon our faith? 4:1
21. Paul urged Timothy to stay in this city___. 1:3
23. The rich are commanded to be___. 6:18
24. Deacons should be worthy of this. 3:8
26. Timothy was to turn away from this chatter. 6:20

Bible Study
CrossWords

1 Timothy

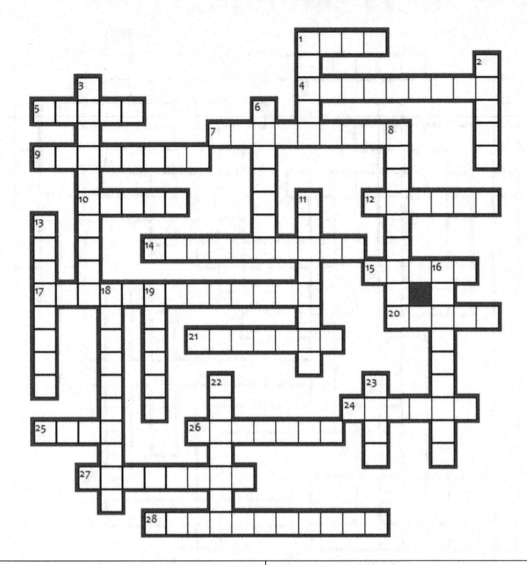

Across   2 Timothy

1. How Paul described his fight to keep his faith. 4:7
4. Timothy was to be on-guard against____. 4:14
5. As men opposed Moses, they will oppose this. 3:8
7. Jesus Christ was____from David. 2:8
9. What times will be like in the last days. 3:1
10. Paul endured so these would be saved. 2:10
12. Paul would be rescued from this to heaven. 4:18
14. We must know the Lord and turn from this. 2:19
15. In time some men will turn their ears to this. 4:4
17. We must pursue this along with faith and love. 2:22
20. He deserted Paul because he loved the world. 4:10
21. How Paul describes Timothy's faith. 1:5
24. Paul asked Timothy to join him suffering for this. 1:8
25. Before this Christ Jesus gave us grace. 1:9
26. How Timothy was to keep Paul's teaching 1:13
27. The faith of men with a mind like this is rejected. 3:8
28. Paul asked Timothy to greet this household. 4:19

Down   2 Timothy

1. This was revealed with the appearance of Jesus. 1:9
2. This was in store for Paul from God. 4:8
3. Timothy was to warn against____ about words. 2:14
6. Do not feel____ when you testify about our Lord. 1:8
8. Jesus Christ did this to death. 1:10
11. Near end times people will love this - not God. 3:4
13. How we should be presented before God. 2:15
16. He wandered away from the truth. 2:17
18. He was one of two who deserted Paul in Asia. 1:15
19. The name of Timothy's mother. 1:5
22. How did Paul remember Timothy? 1:3
23. Timothy was to preach this with great patience. 4:2

Bible Study
CrossWords

2 Timothy

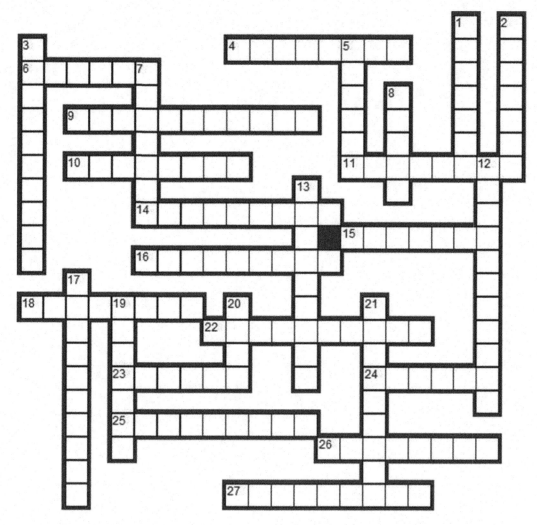

Across   **Titus & Philemon**

4.   Who Paul called his son and said he was useful. P1:10
6.   Titus was to teach in____with sound doctrine. T2:1
9.   Elders followed the____ message they learned T1:9
10. We are to show this toward all men. T3:2
11. This man was also a prisoner in Christ Jesus. P:23
14. Things from the Holy Spirit are____ for everyone. T3:8
15. We are saved through____ by the Holy Spirit. T3:5
16. Heirs of God have been____ by His grace. T3:7
18. This kind of person must be warned only twice. T3:10
22. An elder must be this and love what is good. T1:8
23. Elders should encourage and____ with authority. T2:15
24. We must____ourselves to doing what is good. T3:14
25. Where was Titus to spend the winter with Paul? T3:12
26. With mercy, the____ and love of God saves us. T3:4
27. An elder must be____ with just one wife. T1:6

Down   **Titus & Philemon**

1.   Paul considered Philemon to be his____. P1:17
2.   Many of the circumcised were just____. T1:10
3.   What teaches us to say no to ungodliness? T2:11
5.   We lived in____ and envy, before God's mercy. T3:3
7.   Titus was told not to let anyone____ him. T2:15
8.   Name of the lawyer traveling with Apollos. T3:13
12. People were to be subject to rulers and____. T3:1
13. Paul told Titus to have this in his teaching. T2:7
17. In what things were slaves to be subject to their masters? T2:9
19. Philemon was to be active in____ his faith. P1:6
20. What gave Paul great joy and encouragement? P1;7
21. Philemon made Paul confident because of this. P1:21

Bible Study
CrossWords

Titus & Philemon

HEBREWS

Hebrews 11:1-2

"Now faith is the assurance of things hoped for,
the conviction of things not seen. For by it the
men of old gained approval." NASB

There is disagreement among Bible scholars regarding whether Paul or someone else wrote this letter to the Hebrews. Whoever the author, he placed great emphasis on having faith in the Atonement of Jesus Christ; the blood from an animal sacrifice had been replaced by the blood of Christ.

The superiority of Christianity over Judaism is a theme that runs throughout the letter, comparing the old and the new with faith being a common component. While chapter eleven uses the word faith twenty-eight times to present Old Testament examples of faith the author also points out that it took Christ to provide salvation.

"These were all commended for their faith, yet none of them received what had been promised. God had planned something better for us that only together with us would they be made perfect." Hebrews 11:29

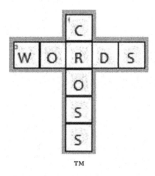

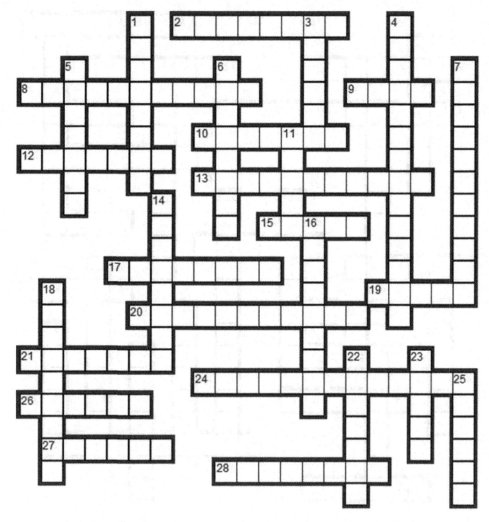

Across   Hebrews 1-3

2. When tempted we should focus our____ on Jesus. 3:1

8. In the beginning, God established these. 1:10
9. This from the Son of God sustains all things. 1:3
10. Jesus suffered when he was____. 2:18
12. Who would become a footstool for Jesus? 1:13
13. What type of spirits are inherent in angels? 1:14
15. Salvation was confirmed by those who____ Jesus. 2:1
17. Those who God has given to Jesus. 2:13
19. Jesus was found more worthy than this man____. 3:3
20. Paul cautioned us to guard against this kind of heart.3:12
21. We will be part of God's house if we hold on to this and to hope. 3:6

24. This would be the scepter of Christ's kingdom. 1:8
26. Spirits who minister to those who will inherit salvation. 2:5
27. Salvation is our only____ from punishment for sin. 3:3
28. Those who were led out of Egypt did this. 3:16

Down   Hebrews 1-3

1. God testified to salvation with these and gifts of the Holy Spirit. 2:4
3. God's____ will last forever. 1:8
4. Jesus Christ is the exact____ of God's being. 1:3
5. There is nothing that is not____ to Jesus. 2:8
6. The disobedient do not enter rest because of this.3:19
7. God spoke to these people through prophets. 1:1
11. Jesus' suffering was to____death for everyone. 2:9
14. Jesus Christ is the____ of God's glory. 1:3
16. Jesus was faithful to the one who____ him. 3:2
18. Salvation was first____ by the Lord. 2:3
22. God is the____ of everything. 3:4

23. Who holds the power of death? 2:14
25. God has____ to us by his Son. 1:1

Bible Study
CrossWords

Hebrews 1-3

Across   Hebrews 4-7

1. Who was considered a priest of God? 7:1

4. Jesus is the source of salvation because he is___ 5 :9

5. Jesus became the___ of a better covenant. 7:22

7. Abraham was promised many of these. 6:14

9. This is as an anchor for our souls. 6:19

10. Faith and hope assure we___ what is promised. 6:12

14. We must be diligent and not become___. 6:12

15. Paul assured the Hebrews that God is not___. 6:10

16. Just like Jesus the word of God is___ and active. 4:12

18. Melchizedek was king of what city? 7:1

20. Knowing the gospel must be combined with this. 4:2

23. Jesus learned obedience because He ___. 5:8

26. Jesus became this because of an oath from God. 7:21

27. God's word does this to our entire being. 4:12

28. Because of the nature and experience of Jesus we can hold___ to our faith. 4:14

Down   Hebrews 4-7

2. Paul thought the truths of God's word should be easy to learn because they are___. 5:12

3. On what day did God rest from His work? 4:4

6. This is impossible for the enlightened who fall away from God. 6:6

8. Everything in___ is seen by God. 4:13

11. The status of God's work after creation. 4:3

12. What prevents us from entering God's rest? 4:6

13. God's rest is called a___-___. 4:8

17. We find this at God's throne. 4:16

19. What God did after finishing his work. 4:4

21. Those who have done this enter God's rest. 4:3

22. What God's word does to our thoughts. 4:12

24. The duration of Jesus Christ's life. 7:24

25. Jesus___ himself as a sacrifice once for the sins of all believers. 7:27

Bible Study CrossWords

Hebrews 4-7

Across	Hebrews 8-10
3.	We should meet and____each other. 10:25
5.	God forgives this and does not remember sins. 8:11
6.	What an enemy of Jesus will become. 10:13
10.	It was necessary for Jesus to be____ a high priest. 8:3
12.	Christ is the____ of a new covenant. 9:15
13.	The Lord's covenant is that He will be our____. 8:10
15.	The Holy Spirit will not _ lawless acts. 10:17
19.	As judge the Lord will____ and repay for sin. 10:30
21.	A sinner's experience at the hands of God. 10:31
24.	We should be confident in the _ of Jesus. 10:37
25.	When Jesus comes everyone will____know him. 8:11
26.	Only this kind of belief will assure our faith. 10:22
27.	We can have this if we do God's will. 10:35
28.	This covenant made the first one obsolete. 8:13

Down	Hebrews 8-10
1.	How Moses referred to the tabernacle he built. 8:5
2.	What the Lord's tabernacle is. 8:2
4.	This from God was fulfilled by Jesus Christ. 10:7
7.	People are made to be this way because of the sacrifice of Jesus. 10:14
8.	High priests on earth serve in a sanctuary that is a copy what is in this place. 8:5
9.	Jesus sacrificed this to make us holy. 10:10
11.	The ministry of Jesus is a superior covenant founded on better____. 8:6
14.	The condition of Jesus as a sacrifice for our sin. 9:14
16.	Where did God say he would put His laws? 8:10
17.	This does not save us if we continue to sin. 10:26
18.	This gave Christ entry to the Most Holy Place. 9:12
20.	Something new that God promised to Israel. 8:8
22.	Christ was a ransom in the new covenant. 9:15
23.	We can hold onto this because God is faithful. 10:23

Bible Study CrossWords

Hebrews 8-10

Across	Hebrews 11-13

1. We should not lose heart when God does this. 12:5
4. Mount Zion was called the ___ Jerusalem. 12:22
5. We should avoid sin and run our race with this. 12:1
7. Our hearts should be strengthened by this. 13:9
8. We should obey these people in authority. 13:17
13. Who by faith was warned about things unseen? 11:7
17. What Abel offered God by faith. 11:4
18. We should not make ___ of the Lord's discipline. 12:5
19. Who avoided death through his faith? 11:5
20. None in the Old Testament received what was ___ .11:39
22. Who was hidden by his parents for 3-months? 11:23
23. Discipline makes our paths this way. 12:13
24. God will never leave us or ___ us. 13:5
25. How often should we offer a sacrifice of praise? 13:15
26. These should be fixed on Jesus. 12:2

Down	Hebrews 11-13

1. Only Jesus has ___ sin to the point of bleeding. 12:4
2. Faith enables us to ___ God formed the universe. 11:3
3. Because God is this to us, we should have no fear. 13:6
4. Marriage should be ___ kept pure. 13:4
6. The ancients were commended for this. 11:1
9. Who by faith was enabled to become a father? 11:11
10. Who received their dead back to life? 11:35
11. We must live in ___ and be holy. 12:14
12. By faith the walls of this city fell. 11:30
14. God is this to all men. 12:23
15. The Lord does this to those he loves. 12:6
16. Do not be ___ immoral or godless like Esau. 12:16
17. Paul referred to Jesus as the great ___. 13:20
20. The prophets could only be made this way through Jesus. 11:40
21. Keep your lives free from the love of this. 13:5

Bible Study CrossWords

Hebrews 11-13

Across   James

7. Every good and perfect gift is from here. 1:17
8. The testing of your faith develops this. 1:3
9. We sometimes pray with the wrong ____ . 4:3
11. Faith is dead if it is not accompanied by this. 2:17
12. If you lack this you should ask God for it. 1:5
13. We must be merciful to receive this. 2:13
14. If someone does this once without keeping the whole law, they are guilty of breaking all of it. 2:10
18. Prayer with this will make a sick person well. 5:15
21. This is promised to those who love God. 2:5

22. Blessed is the man who does this under trial. 1:12
24. We must do this to our neighbor. 2:8
25. When conceived this gives birth to sin. 1:15
26. God called Abraham this because he believed. 2:23
27. We will be judged if we do this to each other. 5:9

28. The____ of life is promised to those who love God.1:12

Down   James

1. Believers in Jesus Christ don't show this. 2:1
2. He who does this is like the wave of the sea 1:6
3. The____ who sow in peace raise a harvest of righteousness 3:18
4. Faith without____ is dead. 2:26
5. Be slow to____because it does not bring a righteous life. 1:19
6. Do this to make the devil flee. 4:7
10. All____ is evil. 4:16

15. The spirit that lives in us____intensely. 4:5
16. God wants us to look after these people when they are in distress. 1:27
17. Wisdom from heaven is first of all____. 3:17
19. Deeds done in____ come from wisdom. 3:13
20. You find this where there is selfish ambition. 3:16
22. God opposes the____. 4:6
23. We should not do this but let our "Yes" be yes and our "No" be no. 5:12

Bible Study CrossWords

James

PETER

1 Peter 3

"Blessed be the Father of our Lord Jesus Christ,
who according to His great mercy has caused us
to be born again to a living hope
through the resurrection of Jesus Christ from the dead." NASB

Peter was one of the chief apostles of the Bible and the head of Jesus' 12 apostles. He was the first disciple that Jesus called and was with Jesus during the transfiguration, was part of Jesus' inner circle and was among the people who received the Holy Spirit on the day of Pentecost.

At his request Peter was crucified upside down because he saw himself as unworthy to die in the same way as Jesus. Jesus gave him the name Cephas, meaning "a rock" in the Syrian language.

Peter's first letter is written to God's "Elect who have been chosen through the foreknowledge of God." He writes about the prospect of persecution of believers because of their identity with Jesus Christ and to respond to it by relying on the grace to be given Christians when Jesus Christ is revealed and to rely on that faith.

"*For you have been born again not of seed that is perishable
but imperishable, that is through the living
and abiding word of God.*" NASB 1 Peter 1:23

TM

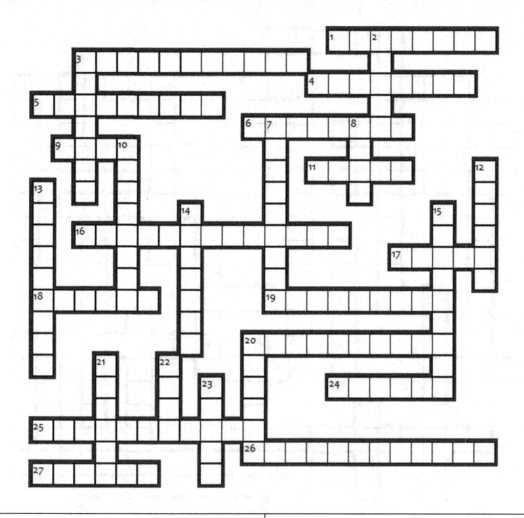

Across 1 Peter	**Down** 1 Peter

Across 1 Peter

1. Christ is our Shepherd and____ of your souls. 2:25
3. We should offer this without grumbling. 4:9
4. Christians should not be ashamed for it is time for____to begin with the family of God. 4:17
5. We should live your lives as____ in reverent fear. 1:17
6. Who spoke of the coming grace and salvation? 1:12
9. We feel this for Christ without seeing him. 1:8
11. What is of greater worth than gold? 1:7
16. The____ of God the Father chose the elect. 1:2
17. God opposes the____but gives grace to the humble. 5:5
18. We should pray because end of all____ is near. 4:7
19. Through faith, this is the goal for our souls. 1:9
20. Wives should be____ to their husbands. 3:1
24. Jesus died in the body but was made alive by the____. 3:18
25. Husbands must be____ with their wives. 3:7
26. The____ of Jesus Christ gives us new birth. 1:3
27. Christ was____ as our Savior before the creation of the world. 1:20

Down 1 Peter

2. How many people were saved from Noah's ark? 1:6
3. We should live in____ with each other. 3:8
7. The eyes of the Lord are on those who are____. 3:12
8. The face of the Lord is against those who d0____. 3:12
10. We are born again through the _ word of God. 1:23
12. We are healed and made righteous by the____ of Jesus. 2:24
13. Peter says we need this kind milk so that we may grow up in salvation. 2:2
14. We can cast all of this on Jesus Christ because he cares for us. 5:7
15. Beauty should not come from outward____. 3:3
20. If we____ because we are Christians, we should praise God that we bear that name. 4:16l
21. Whoever____ in Jesus will never be put to shame. 2:6
22. Christians should always be prepared to respectfully answer why we have this. 3:15
23. We will get this when Jesus Christ is revealed. 1:13

Bible Study CrossWords

1 Peter

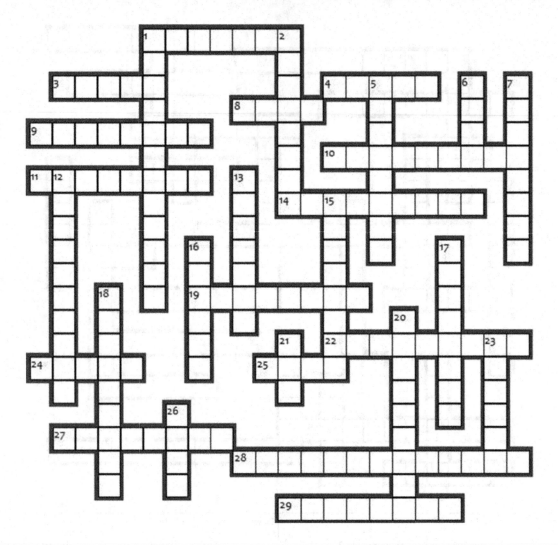

Across	2 Peter
1.	The Lord is____ not wanting us to perish. 3:9
3.	The earth was formed out of this. 2:5
4.	The day of the Lord will come like this. 3:10
8.	Peter said this man wrote with wisdom from God. 3:15
9.	This never had its origin in the will of man. 1:21
10.	This should be added to goodness. 1:5
11.	In the last days____ will follow their own desires. 3:3
14.	False teachers are slaves to this. 2:19
19.	A man is a slave to whatever has____ him. 2:19
22.	False prophets slandered____ beings. 2:10
24.	The Lord knows how to rescue these men from their trials. 2:9
25.	God said, this is my son, whom I ____. 1:17
27.	God has given us great and____promises. 1:4
28.	A new heaven and earth will be the home of ____. 3:13
29.	Add to your faith____. 1:8

Down	2 Peter
1.	This should be added to self-control. 1:6
2.	With the Lord a day is like how many years? 3:8
5.	Some____ people distorted Paul's writings. 3:16
6.	God's____ formed the earth out of water. 3:5
7.	The heavens and earth are____ for fire. 3:7
12.	This is caused by evil desires. 1:4
13.	Ungodly men do this in broad daylight.2:13
15.	Our Lord's____ means salvation. 3:15
16.	Scoffers will say, where is the____ he promised? 3:4
17.	We should be eager to make our____ sure. 1:10
18.	We must add this quality to perseverance. 1:6
20.	Peter wanted his words remembered after this. 1:15
21.	What animal returns to its vomit? 2:22
23.	God did not spare these when they sinned. 2:4
26.	Who was a preacher of righteousness? 2:5

Bible Study CrossWords

2 Peter

Bible Study CrossWords
1 John

Across   1 John

2.   When Jesus does this, we will see him as he is. 3:2
6.   Each____ must be tested before believing them. 4:1
7.   John said many of these had already come. 2:18
9.   Anyone who does not show love remains in____ 3:14
10. This is under the control of the evil one. 5:19
12. What John called Jesus when he testified about him. 1:2
19. If we claim to be without sin, we____ ourselves. 1:8
20. The Holy Spirit and this are one in the same. 5:6
21. The Father sent his Son to be the world's ____. 4:14
22. A name John used for Jesus. 1:1
26. We can obey God's commands because they are not____ . 5:3
27. Paul testified to this kind of life being with Jesus. 1:2
29. A spirit that does not____ Jesus is not from God. 4:3

Down   1 John

1.   This coming from God is greater than from man. 5:9
2.   Love is shown with truth and ____.3:18
3.   Jesus is the____ sacrifice for all sin. 2:2
4.   This describes those who do what is right. 3:7
5.   There is a Spirit of truth and one of ____. 4:6
8.   We must keep ourselves from ____. 5:21
11. The antichrist____ the Father and the Son.2:22
13. Doing the will of God means life . 2:17
14. Being____ of God separates us from the devil. 3:9
15. This does not exist where there is love. 4:18
16. We____ in Jesus because we have his Spirit. 4:13
17. A child of God loves his____and lives in the light. 3:10
18. God calls us this because of his love for us. 3:1
23. This cannot be found in God. 1:5
24. What purifies us from all sin? 1:7
25. He who does what is____ is of the devil. 3:8
28. Who is love? 4:16

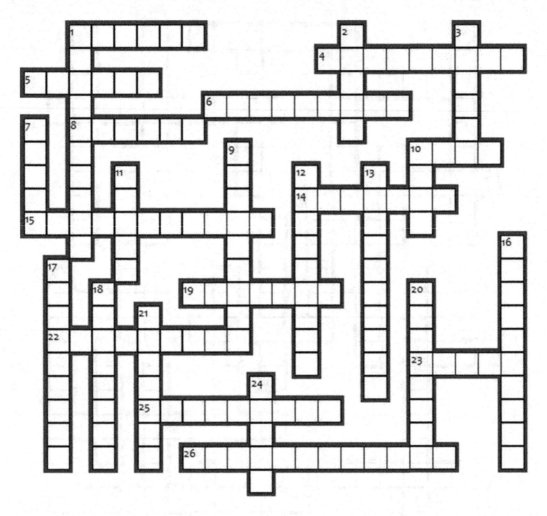

Across   2, 3 John & Jude

1. Who was bound with chains in darkness? J:6
4. Jude was eager to write about this. J:3
5. Who commanded that children walk in truth? 2J:4
6. These people did not acknowledge Jesus Christ as coming in the flesh. 2J:7
8. Anyone who does not continue in the teaching of___does not have God. 2J:9
10. To who was 2John written? 2J:1
14. The Lord destroyed those delivered out of Egypt who did not ____. J:5
15. John encouraged showing this to the brothers. 3J:8
19. What angel disputed with the devil? J:9
22. Gaius was faithful to brothers who were____. 3J:5
23. What was entrusted to the saints? J:3
25. Who was well spoken of by everyone? 3J:12
26. John was pleased about the____of Gaius to truth. 3J:3

Down   2, 3 John & Jude

1. Any deceiver is the same as this. 2J:7
2. Who was the brother of Jude? J:1
3. Anyone who welcomes a deceiver shares in his___work. 2J:11
7. What prophet was the seventh from Adam? J:14
9. The ungodly follow natural ____. J:19
10. Jesus Christ will be with us in truth and ____. 2J3
11. To who was 3John written? 3J:1
12. John said walking in this way is a form of love. 2J:6
13. Who loved to be first and rejected John? 3J:9
16. Those who practice perversion suffer___of eternal fire. J:7
17. John called attention to the___ of Diotrephes. 3J:10
18. We should be this to those who doubt. J:22
20. These people will follow their own ungodly desires.J:18
21. Who will be convicted by the Lord and thousands of holy ones? J:15
24. This will live in us forever. 2J:2

Bible Study CrossWords

2, 3 John & Jude

PROMOTIONAL PUZZLES

Because of a unique format individual BibleStudy CrossWords puzzles stand on the their own. Not requiring an answer grid means the puzzles can be promotional handouts and advertisements with a message, logo and contact information as shown in this sample.

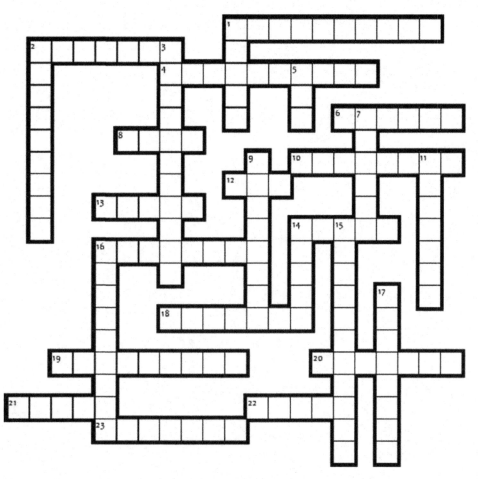

Across	Genesis 6-9
1.	The ___ of heaven opened to create rain. 7:11
2.	Type of wood used to build the ark. 6:14
4.	What did God give Noah as food? 9:3
6.	Who Noah said to be Shem's slave. 9:26
8.	What did God use to recede the waters? 8:1
10.	God wiped every ___ from the earth. 7:4
12.	How many hundred years was Noah? 7:6
13.	The bird sent to check the water? 8:7
14.	The ark was 4-hundred and _ feet long. 6:15
16.	What the animals did after the flood? 8:17
18.	How did the waters react to the wind? 8:1
19.	How were daughters of men viewed? 6:2
20.	Noah prayed for this son's territory. 9:27
21.	Number of each clean animal. 7:2
22.	The leaf the dove brought to the ark? 8:11
23.	What month did the ark come to rest? 8:4

Down	Genesis 6-9
1.	How many days did it rain? 7:4
2.	God saw that people were ___. 6:12
3.	Day the ark came to rest. 8:4
5.	Son who fathered Canaan. 9:18
7.	Where the ark came to rest. 8:4
9.	What did Noah plant? 9:20
11.	What was the sign of God's covenant? 9:13
14.	Never again will God use this to destroy the earth. 9:11
15.	What God used to destroy life on earth. 6:17
16.	What were covered with over 20-feet of water? 7:20
17.	Who were the heroes of old, men of renown? 6:4

(MESSAGE)

YOUR LOGO &
CONTACT INFORMATION

BibleStudy CrossWords 2020

Contact Bob Meister for more information and to request personalized sample:
479-655-4518 / church7@cox.net

Printed in the United States
By Bookmasters